HOW GOD GIVES US CHOCOLATE

CHOCOLATE

CE

COCOA CANYON

BOARD THE
Chocolate Express
HERE!

Library of Congress Catalog Card Number 91-65270
©1991, The STANDARD PUBLISHING Company, Cincinnati, Ohio
Division of STANDEX INTERNATIONAL Corporation. Printed in U.S.A.

HOW GOD GIVES US CHOCOLATE

written by Henrietta D. Gambill

illustrated by Jan Arness

God gives us sweet, brown chocolate
to eat and enjoy.

We can have chocolate candy, cake,
ice cream, pie, and even chocolate milk!

Chocolate comes from only one place in the whole world—down near the equator in the middle of the earth.

The chocolate trees grow there in the jungles, where it's very hot, wet, and sunny all the time!

God gives the jungle lots of rain, warm sunshine, and good, rich soil.

Then the chocolate trees begin to grow tiny buds on their trunks and branches.

The buds burst open and tiny,
little flowers appear.
 They bloom for a short time,
then they fall off.
 And where each flower was,
a small pod starts to grow.

The pods grow big and long. They soon look like melons hanging on the chocolate trees.

Inside the pods are lots and lots of white seeds. Yes, chocolate seeds are white at first. Later they turn chocolate brown.

At harvest time, workers use big, sharp knives to cut the pods from the trees, open them, and place the white beans in the sun to dry.

Slowly, very slowly, the white beans turn
a rich, red-brown color.

When the chocolate beans are dry, they are put into large bags. And off they go to the chocolate factory.

COCOA BEANS

COCOA BEANS

TO FACTORY

At the factory, the chocolate beans are cleaned and separated. Little beans together and big beans together.

All of the beans, big and little, are cooked by roasting. As they roast, the shells crack and fall off.

Roasting causes the chocolate beans to turn a dark, dark brown color.

Then, at last, the smell of chocolate comes from the dark brown beans for the first time.

Next, the roasted chocolate beans are rolled between huge, big rollers. The beans crack into thousands and thousands of little pieces called nibs.

The little nibs don't stay nibs for very long.

They are ground and smashed, and squished and squashed, by another big machine until there's nothing left but thick, dark, chocolate syrup.

Sometimes milk and powdered sugar are added to the syrup to make it taste even better.

Now comes the most important step in making chocolate. It's called conching.

The conching machines have big, heavy rollers that beat the chocolate and move it back and forth, back and forth, for several days!

The longer the conching time, the better the chocolate tastes.
Can you see why conching is the most important step in making chocolate?

After conching for several days, the
creamy chocolate is poured into molds.
Some candy molds are big, some small,
some shaped like rabbits, or even a ball.

The molds are cooled, and the chocolate shapes harden.

Then slowly and carefully, the molds turn over and empty the brown chocolate treats.

The chocolate bars and special things
are then wrapped in paper, put in boxes,
and sent to the stores.
They are ready for you to buy and eat!

Thank You, God,
for chocolate so sweet,
dark and rich,
what a wonderful treat!